Endorser

"*R.E.M.O.T.E.* is a book whose time has come. Marci Powell knows whereof she writes, and hands out expert and entertaining advice to all who must, or choose to, work from 'anywhere' but in the office." -Lynne Reid Banks

"A book that provides valuable insights, best practices, and practical solutions on how to thrive when working remotely." -Dr. Andy DiPaolo, Executive Director Emeritus, Stanford Center for Professional Development

"Distributed workforces can no longer be 'remote' from learning, engagement, and storytelling. Marci Powell, a leading expert in digital learning and collaboration, provides great models, strategies, and resources for making the 'distance' disappear! A must read for EveryDay Learning." -Elliott Masie, Chair of The Learning CONSORTIUM at The Masie Center

"Marci Powell's new book is full of insights. I rely upon those insights heavily in the day-to-day of running my organization." -Paul Bardack, Executive Director, Maryland Small Business Development Center

"*R.E.M.O.T.E.* is a practical guide for any professional working at a distance or any manager that supervises remote workers. Marci Powell contributes her decades of experience building successful and productive global teams. This must-read book offers guidance in building healthy remote teams, in practicing high-powered prioritization, producing high-performance level results, and managing team expectations. Professionals who desire to be visible, engaged, and productive in their organizations while working remotely will appreciate the invaluable ideas and recommendations in this book." -Dr Susan C. Aldridge, Executive Higher Education Consultant and President (Ret.), Drexel University Online

"'At a distance' guru, Marci Powell is right on the money. In just a couple of hours of reading, you'll gain valuable insights that can have a significant long-term impact on your organization's future." -Reggie Smith III, Ph.D., CEO, USDLA

R.E.M.O.T.E.

R.E.M.O.T.E.

R.E.M.O.T.E.

Leverage the Distance and Achieve Excellence When Working Remotely

By Marci Powell

Marci Powell

For general information about our products or services, please contact the author at marci@marcipowell.co.

Marci Powell

Library of Congress Cataloging-in-Publication Data is on file with the publisher.

Publishers Cataloging-in-Publication Data
R.E.M.O.T.E.: Leverage the Distance and Achieve Excellence When Working Remotely
116 pages cm.
ISBNs: 978-1-7353292-0-8 Paperback
        978-1-7353292-1-5 ePub
        978-1-7353292-2-2 Mobi
        978-1-7353292-3-9 Audiobook

Printed in the United States of America

Table of Contents

Prologue

The Wilson Dam in northern Alabama was—at one time—the world's largest one-lock dam. When my husband and I were a young, newly married couple, we were taking an evening stroll around the perimeter of the dam when I noticed a strange-looking cage on the bank. The cage resembled the kind a diver would get into when researching sharks.

An odd place for a shark, I wondered what purpose it could serve in the middle of the United States, absolutely nowhere near the ocean. The lock keeper was nearby, so we walked over to ask him what it was all about. His reply was a lesson I will never forget.

He shared with us that the lock was so deep that the engineers and mechanics would not go down to work on the turbines without being in one of the shark cages because the catfish were so huge that they could swallow a man whole.

As I imagined the small, two-inch-long catfish in my aquarium or those in my lake at home, the shock on my face was obvious. He confirmed my reaction by continuing his story. The 94-foot lock sits in 500 feet of water, and catfish grow to the size of their environment. So, with such an enormous "tank," the catfish had room to grow to an unimaginable size.

Thanks to the digital age, the traditional four walls of an office or classroom have vanished in order to create an unlimited virtual environment. Companies and individuals can grow as big as they want to be. People can work from home or anywhere.

Over the last twenty-five years—with a dramatic increase in the last few—we've seen a paradigm shift taking place as many organizations enable remote work. The shift has been exponentially propelled due to the Coronavirus (COVID-19) pandemic—one bright outcome in an otherwise trying time.

The trend to work from home (WFH) or work from anywhere (WFA) has become the next-generation workplace, with many employees becoming new-collar workers. Some call it the "laptop lifestyle." It is what many people dream of when asked about their perfect job: the ability to work in an environment that lends to an individual's creative nature and inspires them personally, where they can work from anywhere. This has proven to result in greater productivity, and often, in less time. Is working remotely a truly effective way to foster productivity and increase growth overall? Not only is it effective, it is ideal.

The benefits to businesses are tremendous. Being able to work remotely allowed me to move from living in the seventh-largest city in America, to life on a 20-acre farm about 100 miles from Dallas. For me, the back porch is my office; the swing is my desk chair. A private lake surrounded by the breathtaking beauty of nature is my view as I work. I enjoy the flexibility and freedom of remote work, but the benefits don't stop there.

Individual Benefits

There are many advantages to working in a remote environment. It can be extremely productive and especially rewarding. Both the individual and the organization can see the return on this "work from anywhere" style.

For an individual, remote work enables a person to have a greater margin for life. This means a healthier work/life balance. In some cases, being able to work from home widens the opportunity pool when previously living in a rural location limited the type of opportunities that exist in more densely-populated areas. It allows you to find your passion to do what you love, and to get paid while doing it.

To be able to work and learn from anywhere allows you to travel or enjoy living wherever you want. For me, I have done both. Traveling to many beautiful places, experiencing so many cultures, and working with amazing people from around the world has been priceless. Likewise, the flexibility to live where I choose has been a blessing—especially at times when my husband was transferred. My job did not have to change because we had to move.

Since 1989 and 1998 respectively, my husband and I have worked remotely. For many years, our offices have been just across the hall from one another. Unlike my remote job where I could live anywhere in the world, my husband had to live in a defined geographic territory based on the location of his customers or the teams he managed. Regardless, remote work has given both of us a better quality of life with different opportunities and different companies.

We have been close enough to discuss what we want to do for lunch on any given day. Rather than kissing each other goodbye for the day and then spending hours apart, we have been able to remain close, and even be there when the kids got home from school. This offered us a better quality of family life too.

Time is another benefit when working remotely. No commute! For us, commuting took two hours a day Monday through Thursday, and three hours on Fridays. Gaining that time back allowed us to adjust our working hours to increase productivity, as well as to accommodate for family time and energy levels. Being free from the distractions of unnecessary, lengthy conversations that take place at the office also increases the daily productivity time.

Financially, there is a smaller investment in work attire, wear and tear to personal vehicles, fuel, and a quieter environment that you can control. You can choose a variety of break times that can help you focus and stay on track. All of these advantages are only a few of the reasons why remote work is a more effective way to operate an entire workforce.

What's in It for the Organization?

Working from anywhere in the world offers equally as many benefits to an organization as it does for an individual. To start, a lot of organizations are moving toward enabling working remotely because they find substantial savings from a business perspective— specifically savings on real estate. Having a team of remote employees dramatically reduces brick-and-mortar location costs including rent, utilities, and many other overhead expenses.

According to a Forbes Magazine article,[1] in the last decade, Aetna, an American insurance giant "shed 2.7 million square feet of office space, and as a result saved $78 million."[2] Using their own Telework Savings Calculator, Global Workplace Analytics (GWA)[3] calculated that allowing full-time remote work can save companies between $20,000 and $37,000 per employee, per year.

IBM saves $50 million annually, while Sun Microsystem saves $68 million. By reviewing over 4000 studies and

1   https://www.forbes.com/sites/andrealoubier/2017/07/20/benefits-of-telecommuting-for-the-future-of-work/#467e482316c6

2   https://www.forbes.com/sites/jeannemeister/2013/04/01/flexible-workspaces-another-workplace-perk-or-a-must-have-to-attract-top-talent/#298ec08b2ce7

reports, GWA gathered other interesting statistics to identify additional benefits.[3]

Best Buy, British Telecom, Dow Chemical, and many others show that teleworkers are 35-40% more productive.[3] A Stanford University study[4] conducted by Professor Nicolas Bloom focusing on China's biggest travel agency, Ctrip, found that enabling remote work saw productivity increase by 22%, while employee turnover rates fell by over 50%. WFH/WFA reduces absenteeism and improves retention of good employees.

The savings alone are enormous, but it is equally beneficial for a business that is looking for quality employees. Offering a remote-work option gives an organization a larger pool of potential candidates. They can cast their net wider in the search from a local reach to a grander scale where they may have more qualified individuals apply, who live anywhere in the world.

Likewise, WFH/WFA policies enable an organization to expand customer reach to be more direct, and enables them to get the cream of the crop of employees, both of which can ultimately yield great results on a *grow big* scale.

Additionally, the opportunity for online education to be included in an organization's offerings, will allow remote employees to easily re-skill or upskill. Like catfish,

---

3   https://globalworkplaceanalytics.com/pros-cons

4   https://www.youtube.com/watch?v=oiUyyZPIHyY

people can grow to the size of their environment, and maybe as big as they dream.

Challenges

However, with the increase in a remote workforce, and the flexibility and freedom it brings, comes a new set of challenges. It is vital to adapt so you can do great work from anywhere. Transitioning from a traditional environment to a remote one demands a new approach with some adjustments.

Organizations and individuals need a strategy for remote work. Working outside of the conventional office, employees can feel disconnected or isolated. Communication can break down. Inevitably there will be technology hiccups. Managers can be uncertain of how to oversee productivity or measure their employees' performance. Time management is paramount because it is extremely easy to either not work enough or to work too much. It takes knowing how to manage yourself and your remote teams in order to be the most productive. Done right, an organization will benefit greatly by being effective and efficient. Done wrong, and an organization can suffer operationally.

Finally

With the marketplace trend that includes a remote-work structure to best serve the next-generation workforce, there is an opportunity to stay in front while improving productivity and the overall quality of life for both the employee and the organization. Much like the catfish in the story, working in a remote environment can help you *grow big* as an employee, a learner, and as an organization.

This book is designed to be a quick read, yet a tool that helps you focus and apply key principles for remote work; where you can learn to work remotely to achieve the highest level of productivity and joy. Each chapter will focus on one letter of the word **REMOTE**: **R**eadiness & Rhythm, **E**ngagement, **M**anagement of Self and Team, **O**perating at a High Level of Productivity, **T**rust & Team, and finally, **E**xcellence.

You deserve to be able to work remotely and accomplish great things for your organization and your personal life. You can work, learn, and live from anywhere!

CHAPTER 1

Readiness & Rhythm

Our first year at the farm, I found one particular view from my back-porch office extremely awe-inspiring. With an occasional glance toward our 2-acre pond we call "the lake," I get to watch blue herons and egrets find a home to build a nest. I see red cardinals, blue jays, hummingbirds, woodpeckers, and other birds of a variety of colors snack at our bird feeders. I have even watched two Texas river otters play-wrestle on our pier. But one of the most fascinating things I have observed in nature has been the water striders.

These half-inch-long insects have a thin body with three sets of legs, and they sort of look like mosquitos. For certain, it wasn't their beauty that caught my attention. Water striders, also known as pond skaters, are one of the most interesting and enjoyable aquatic creatures to observe. I would sit on my pier and watch these incredible insects actually walk on water.

With unimaginable precision, throngs of water striders would form a line to play "follow the leader" types of activities. Their straight lines sliding across the water's surface would quickly become moving circles and "infinity" formations.

At one point, three throngs of water striders made a moving Venn diagram. Seriously. In the blink of an eye, they would change direction from clockwise to counterclockwise. It was astonishing to observe. It was like watching the artistic Olympic synchronized swimming competition. I was captivated by their creativity and the way they worked together especially with great speed. How I wish I had taken videos of it.

When I think about these amazing insects, I see several things that can apply to working remotely: creativity, outstanding teamwork, agility, speed, synchronized execution, precision, and flow.

While this is what we want in any work environment, it can be done easily and beautifully when working remotely. Whether you are part of a remote team or a freelancer, you can still move with brilliant performance.

Challenges and Concerns

When it comes to remote employment, however, there are four major things people seem to struggle with.

Firstly, there's always the fear of the unknown and the fear of overcoming concerns. If you are choosing to work remotely you might have concerns about the transition. If you have been told you will be working remotely two or three days a week because the office is downsizing its physical space, you may not be able to fathom how this will be possible when you have worked co-located for so long. If you supervise a team or teams, the idea that you are going to have people that report to you who are working remotely may cause great concern.

Many times, people have said to me, "I could never work remotely because I would never get anything done, and I would always be distracted or interrupted, or I would go stir-crazy." On the other hand, I also hear people say the opposite: "I could never work remotely because I wouldn't know how to stop working for the day. It would invade my personal life." Truthfully, if not done correctly, WFH can turn into either of those realities.

Secondly, people and some businesses struggle with fear of the unknown. They have never experienced WFH/WFA. They don't know what they don't know, and they don't know where to begin or how to go about it. They wonder, "What does successful WFH/WFA look like?"

Thirdly, there are seven deadly words that inhibit progress: "We've never done it that way before." That will always hurt any organization. Using this argument is weak, but more importantly it is deadly. It can cripple forward movement for any organization. It can impede personal growth and development. It can hinder innovation and productivity. Working from Home (WFH) and working from anywhere (WFA) is a large part of the future workplace and should be considered sooner rather than later.

Fourth and finally, I hear some say, "Okay, I am in for working remotely, but I have no idea where to start or how to get going." More often now since the social-distancing impact than in previous years, people who have started working remotely have overcome the fear, but are still figuring out the best way to flourish remotely.

Flexibility is a treasure when working remotely, but self-discipline is the key to ensuring that you are highly productive and balancing your time. Working remotely makes it too easy to allow distractions or to keep working to the point of losing a healthy balance. Without the irritating commute that consumed your time, it makes it too easy to be at your desk three hours earlier than normal and to work right through lunch without changing out of your sleep attire.

It is extremely important to strike balance. When working out of your home, there is always something personal that needs to be done in addition to accomplishing work for your job. Most homes always have something that needs to be fixed or cleaned, kids are active, and distractions are all around to tempt you to divide your focus away from work.

On the flip side, some people find it hard to disconnect from their remote work and end up checking emails while they are on holidays, trying to keep the work "caught up." Something comes to mind, and the person intends to get that one thing done so they do not forget it, and two hours later they look up, exhausted from getting caught in the flow. Working from home is not supposed to be a "fun day" to just do what you want and be available by email, but it is also not overworking 10-12 hour days and on weekends without any down time.

Readiness

Going remote means making yourself and/or your team ready to work remotely—it takes a different mindset. You need a good space or environment. A system lets you be as productive as possible while maintaining a healthy work/life balance. You need the right equipment and tools. With the stage set, you need discipline, focus and a plan.

Distractions can be turned into something that can boost your productivity. It is a matter of readiness and finding your rhythm. For organizations, it is important to define a remote-working strategy that includes aligning policies, procedures, and simplified processes to a remote workforce. Create an organizational culture that fosters thriving productivity.

Whether planning at the organizational or individual level, preparation is paramount. Like water striders, working remotely can look like a well-orchestrated dance of precision—you will glide through a workday.

Define Your Space/Environment

What do you want your environment to look like, and what will it take to keep distractions to a minimum? Do you have children at home? School closures because of COVID-19 made working remotely even more difficult with normally quiet parts of the day being flooded by bored children who hungered for attention or weren't always getting along. It can get quite crazy and stop productivity.

Where can you get away from the chaos? How can you control the chaos and still be productive? Define your space and a system that everyone in the household can follow. Find a space where you can work free from distractions as much as possible and yet not feel completely isolated.

For me, that means switching spaces depending on my work activity and who is in the house. As I have said, my favorite spot is working from my back-porch swing. I love looking out at nature while I work. It helps me regroup my thoughts or marinate on an idea.

When I am on video calls, I have created a space with a nice background that doesn't have my bed showing. It sets a tone that looks more business-like. When the kids are around, I find a quiet place and lock the door. While it is easy to set up activities for older kids, with smaller children, someone needs to watch them. For me, the value of having two people work from home has been the ability to take turns. When the kids are home, we arrange our schedules to accommodate everyone. It is also amazing how much work can be done after the kids have gone to bed, or before they get up.

If you need—and are energized by social interaction beyond what you get by using video conferencing—consider using a co-working space. Some remote workers will go to one of these remote-work hub spaces a day or two a week just to have human interaction and to bounce ideas off of others.

Defining your space takes a little bit of creativity if you are able to travel while working remotely. When in Europe, for example, I would occasionally take tours in the morning through lunch, and then work with the American team in the afternoon and evening. Having flexibility to adjust hours is great, but you have to be more creative about defining your workspace. Sometimes that means finding a quiet place to do video conferences. Many nights it meant working from the hotel room, depending on the time zones.

As long as there is a good internet connection and access to the tools or files needed, you can work from anywhere—including the beach of a remote island, a café on the streets of a European market square, or at a cabin in a rainforest. It simply depends on whether or not you have to meet with co-workers or customers that day.

Technologies

To flourish remotely, you need to start figuring out where, when, and how you will work, and you will need to ensure that the right technologies are in place. Most likely, your job will require high-speed internet. It could be easy to find, as many metropolitan cities have huge bandwidths available to the home.

Outside a metroplex, however, it could be hard and take some creativity to find. At our farm, we had trouble finding anything with more than a ½ mb uplink and a 3 mb downlink. Try video conferencing with those speeds—it's not going to happen. We finally found a WIFI (MiFi mobile hotspot) provider who offered at least 15mb up and down. While it wasn't anywhere near what we enjoyed in the larger city, it works good enough for the two of us to work remotely and to be on different video calls at the same time.

In addition to video conferencing and streaming, other types of work we need to accomplish might require sufficient bandwidth: document sharing, collaborative tools, sales or client support systems, and more. You have to be able to function in full-capacity business mode to work from home. If you want to work from anywhere beyond your home office, get a MiFi to take with you that lets you pull from cell phone towers even in more remote areas.

If you travel, be aware of where there are limitations and adjust your schedule accordingly. When I participate in a video call while riding in a car, I have to know where the dead spots are and work around them. Get the right tools and support set up to keep technology frustrations to a minimum.

When the response to the Coronavirus forced so many to work from home, I talked to several people who couldn't function because of the limit IT had placed on their access. They couldn't get to the files they needed in order to do their jobs. My friend Sandi found she could not access the Internet on her company-issued device. It wasn't a problem with the laptop, instead it was because IT had restricted access outside of the company's building. Not only that, but it wouldn't allow her to download or print anything. Sandi was limited from the start. It was impossible to function at a minimum, much less at full capacity.

Barriers to working outside of the conventional office need to be removed (without compromising data security). Organizations MUST figure out the best technology and access approach, but it is equally important to think through other processes that can be detrimental to productivity for those not in the conventional office.

Look at what access remote workers will need in order to be able to do their jobs. Consider what technologies are needed to do business, to collaborate, and to have social interaction. Besides office productivity tools and data security, you will need communication and collaboration channels to promote connecting, teamwork, and to prevent isolation. Perhaps project software is needed to help everyone be on the same page in regards to timelines and deliverables. There are even apps that help you focus and block distractions.

When I first joined a board of directors for an organization, I found that for board meetings, the executive team and local board members would gather at headquarters while the rest of the board was remote. After a year of struggling to hear everyone over video conferencing calls, and hopefully not missing anything important, I felt things needed to change.

When I became board chair, I attended in-person and worked to make sure the environment was optimal for everyone including the board members who joined the meetings remotely. It wasn't until I made the shift to have everyone join calls remotely that meetings became the best for every individual. It leveled the playing field by putting all board members on equal footing. Nobody missed what was said, nor did they miss seeing who was talking—which had happened all the time before when multiple people were in one room and the camera was not a wide-angle lens.

Video conferencing (VC) chats are optimal for helping people feel equally connected. I cannot say enough about it. Social communicative tools like VC help establish connections, making social distancing seem to disappear. Video conferencing plays a key role in recreating face-to-face meetings as closely as possible.

If you want to emulate being in the office, use VC for meetings and have huddles when you can. Make sure that everyone understands good video conferencing etiquette. Once your space and technologies are ready, it is time to set a work time and style that works for you.

Rhythms

When are you most creative? What is your peak productivity time? When do you mentally move the fastest and are the most on-task? When is your brain least productive? What works for you as an individual? As a team?

Water striders are very fast. They can move at "speeds of a hundred body lengths per second. To match them, a 6-foot-tall person would have to swim at over 400 miles an hour" (National Geographic; Cool Green Science). [5] Oh, that we could all move that fast! While water striders move with productive speed and accuracy beyond what is possible for a person, we can still optimize how fast we work. I call it "finding your rhythm."

I am most productive early in the morning. So, if I get a good night's rest, I can start at 5 or 6 am and

---

5   https://blog.nature.org/science/2017/04/10/7-cool-facts-water-striders-skippers-pond-skaters-weird-nature/

work all the way to lunch, producing like you wouldn't believe. Things are coming out as fast as I can get them done. I have sharper focus when I work within my prime rhythm, especially when the task involves greater creativity.

Conversely, my daughter has horrible productive potential in the morning hours. But if you ask her to start working on a project at 8 or 9 pm, she will go until 2 or 3 am and produce abundantly. She is at her peak performance between 11 pm and 2 am. During her childhood, she would start doing her homework at 10 pm and it would drive me nuts because I had to get her up for school early the next morning. While that was our battle, she had found her rhythm. It works for her. Part of finding that rhythm for yourself is finding what works for your body. When is your brain the most turned on? Discover the environment that enables that rhythm to give you that productive beat.

While writing this chapter yesterday, I began at 5 am and worked at a very fast pace. I was very pleased with my progress. Then, a couple of hours past a working lunch (not something you should get in the habit of doing), my productivity rate slowed to a snail's pace. After struggling for nearly an hour on one small part of the chapter, I realized I had been working for over eight hours straight. I had passed my optimal productivity time. My body got to the point where it would take me three hours to do something that normally would have only taken 20 minutes. I had pushed myself past the point of staying productive. In finding your rhythm, not only do you find your best time to work, you must also know when to stop.

The Remote Mindset

To thrive when working remotely takes a "remote mindset." You must be flexible to handle whatever the day brings you. Here, more than ever, it takes a resilient and agile mindset. To work remotely you need the ability to spring forward when change or challenges present themselves; to be flexible and able to recover quickly when things affect the process. You need agility—the ability to move quickly and with ease—as well as the ability to think and understand quickly. Much like athletes or dancers exemplify physical agility, mental agility is the key for involving critical thinking and responding with a high level of alertness to any situation.

In one of his blogs, Matthew L. Miller, the Director of Science Communications for The Nature Conservancy comments on striders saying, "The water skipper's legs are so buoyant they can support fifteen times the insect's weight without sinking. Even in a rainstorm or in waves, the strider stays afloat. The strider's legs do more than repel water; they're also configured to allow efficient and rapid movement across the surface."[6] A

---

6   https://blog.nature.org/science/2017/04/10/7-cool-facts-water-striders-skippers-pond-skaters-weird-nature/

remote mindset enables you to work efficiently and move rapidly even when things get tough.

Resilient and agile workers not only function autonomously, but also know how to work on remote teams. Creativity and critical thinking combined with great communication and collaboration skills enable you to think outside the box, innovate, and problem solve. Achieving maximum productivity is like walking on water. Working in highly collaborative teams takes precision. Even in a rainstorm, or in waves, the strider stays afloat. Working remotely demands the same level of responsiveness, agility, and resilience. How quickly and smoothly can you adjust or move?

With a remote mindset, being able to see the positive, bounce back, stretch, overcome challenges, and expand—all of these lead to success. Have a mental reservoir of strength. As the digital transformation of the next-generation workplace begins to take shape, both agility and resilience must work together. Work/life balance and work/life integration allows remote employees to work on their own time, at their own speed. Having a remote mindset and a culture where we can quickly shift and understand what is needed to enable productivity is highly important.

When working remotely, you will have "rock star" days where agility and resilience shines through and you are at a high-performance level. But you will also have frustrating days. The good news is that being remote means you will have fewer days where you exhaust yourself responding to everyone else in the office, only to discover at the end of the day that you didn't accomplish any of the tasks on your list. Regardless of the type of day you have, readiness and rhythm will help you keep balance and navigate through. Whether progress is tracked through metrics-driven or other measurable values, hold yourself accountable so that your performance levels are where they should be, especially in a flexible work environment.

The right mindset will set you up for tremendous impact and enable you to make a significant contribution to your organization and to society as a whole. It all begins by making the conscientious choice to be at the top of your game, to have the right attitude, to make sure you are constantly developing yourself (upskilling in both soft and hard skills), and by being resilient and agile as things evolve.

Final Thoughts on Readiness & Rhythm

One of the more interesting facts I learned about water striders was the extreme level to which they can adapt to different environments. It's called polymorphism. Some species of water striders have wings only when they're likely to need them. It is the mechanism that enables a parent to have one brood of young without wings, while the next brood has them. This allows water striders to be very adaptable to changing water and habitat conditions.

Working remotely can be a challenge, especially when you first start out. It is a new environment, with a change in conditions compared to a conventional office. With readiness and finding your rhythm, you can flourish—especially if you are good at being adaptable to whatever comes your way.

CHAPTER 2

Engagement

My daughter-in-law Laura starts her remote workday with a yoga class taught by one of her colleagues through video conferencing. Next, she prepares breakfast and snaps a picture of her plate and the recipe to share with her company's cooking club social media group. She laughs at some of their humorous posts. Some of her colleagues are getting quite creative in quick-meal preparation. A quick glance at the pet Slack channel gives her plenty of things she can comment on to build camaraderie during the upcoming VC team meetings. Even as she begins her workday, Laura already feels connected to her co-workers and knows how to engage across the teams she manages.

One of the most frustrating issues during COVID-19 was the isolation people felt from having to practice social distancing. Humans are social creatures. Regardless of how much or how little you prefer being around people, you still need interaction. One of the biggest challenges in working remotely, especially in working from home, is feeling isolated. Without deliberate best practices, remote workers can feel disconnected and find the lack of camaraderie overwhelming. This can lead to a lack of motivation. Laura's company found a way to address this challenge.

For certain, it takes adjusting, but just like finding your rhythm, you can find your system for feeling connected. Like Laura's company, some were quite creative during the pandemic. Others who have been WFH and WFA movement for years, have been perfecting how to drive engagement and overcome these challenges for a long time.

While it is nice not to have your lunch stolen from the breakroom refrigerator, you can miss the interaction that naturally happens there. Water-cooler chats are gone. You can't stop by the office of a co-worker to ask a quick question or say, "Let's grab a quick bite." Encounters such as these cannot happen. The camaraderie can disappear when everyone is remote. Even worse, if only some are remote and others are at the office, those in the office grow closer while those working remotely can feel left out or cheated.

On the other hand, some remote employees do not like being away from the hub of activity in terms of office politics, management, and intellectual exchanges. Others worry that not being in the hubbub of activity will have a negative impact on their career advancement. Being at a distance can lead to lack of engagement and a lack of cohesive communication in both directions unless it is managed properly.

Make the Distance Disappear

For those working remotely, you need to make the distance seemingly disappear. It should feel as though there is no distance between those co-located and those working remotely.

Regardless of your reasons for working remotely, everyone should feel connected and have a way to socialize. But how do you create a connected environment that emulates being together in the same room? How do you build camaraderie?

I have had the blessing of working for several technology companies, which organically leads to using digital tools to connect. I have participated in quite a few superb activities of engagement throughout the years, but I have been very impressed by how well Laura's company adapted during the pandemic.

With a flexible working policy, employees can choose their working environment. Laura generally works from her company headquarters in Austin and occasionally works remote throughout the week. The pandemic forced everyone to work from home and consequentially, they became more creative. It proved socialization can easily be emulated even at a distance.

Covey

Dr. Stephen R. Covey was an eminent American educator, author, businessman, and keynote speaker.

One of his most popular books is *The 7 Habits of Highly Effective People*. He is the perfect example of learning how to make the distance disappear.

For years, long before Skype or Zoom existed and the majority of people even knew what video conferencing was, my remote job was to enlighten people about VC, explain potential applications, and teach the best practices. So, when Dr. Covey began transitioning from delivering hundreds of keynote addresses each year in person, to delivering these speeches over video conferencing, I was called in to help.

I flew to Utah to meet with him and his team at his office. A dedicated VC room had been set up with the optimal viewing background. Working with his assistant, I picked out the clothes he would wear to look best on camera.

When I met with Dr. Covey, we focused on the differences between delivering speeches in-person and over video. I provided him with a quick guide in VC etiquette and how to engage the audience at a distance. I called it *7 Habits of Highly Effective Speakers over Video Conferencing*. He chuckled at the title I had made just for him, and his wide smile warmed my heart.

We discussed the importance of engaging his audience right in the beginning. When it was time for his keynote, I observed as I sat off camera. Before he even started his presentation, he addressed the virtual audience saying, "Will the gentleman sitting right there in the green jacket, would you come to the microphone?" The man walked up and stood before the microphone and Dr. Covey said, "First of all, I love your hair. Next time you get a haircut will you mail me some? I can glue it on." Dr. Covey patted his bald head and everyone laughed. Immediately, he effectively engaged his audience right away, just as he was coached to do. Just because you are not physically in the same location does not mean you can't seem like you are.

The Dinghy Effect

A dinghy is a small boat that is tethered to a big ship. It has its purpose, but essentially it is ignored until it is needed. The remote worker can feel like this at times, when they are away from the hubbub of the daily grind. Remote workers can end up feeling isolated, disengaged and disconnected. Eventually this will lead to a lack of motivation.

Many remote workers can feel "out of sight, out of mind." This can have a negative impact on their career advancement. If you feel that no one even thinks of you, you will begin to doubt your worth and your overall purpose on the team, and in the organization. Also, some remote people need the energy of others around them and they thrive on that. How do you eliminate that distance, or make it transparent?

Eliminate what I call the "dinghy effect" by practicing the principles of engagement. Focus on how to keep the employees in the loop and provide them an environment where they can thrive. Make remote employees feel as though they are connecting through collaboration. Healthy remote environments foster connecting through technology by sharing desktops, audio calls, and video calls—always interacting and working together in a "huddle" of some type. Rather than walking into another person's office physically, you can huddle digitally.

Prevent the dinghy effect by making the distance disappear. It is important to remove the isolation and the feeling of being invisible. Just as important, you will need to think about the things that make you feel engaged within your own company, understanding that remote teams may not be able to engage in the same way.

Get Creative

Water-cooler chats happen when employees have conversations in passing that are casual and personal in nature. This helps them to bond individually and build teams. Without them, you can feel disconnected. Recreate that experience easily with virtual water-cooler chats by purposefully setting up activities like Laura's company does with their cooking club and pet channel. One major advantage of replacing in-person experiences this way is that you can eliminate the negative side of lengthy water-cooler chats with streamlined activities that are timesaving yet effective.

Besides social media interactions, add a few minutes to the beginning of weekly huddles for fun conversation. Set the stage for your employees to share meals virtually. Not working lunches, but actual breakroom or "let's grab lunch" style video conferences. You may want a special huddle on a Friday where everyone just shares what cool things are happening in their part of the world.

If you enable employees to work on their own innovative ideas, it's a great thing to talk about in a VC chat. Building rapport needs to be intentionally created in order to grow the team. When you build your teams, you get to know what they are really good at, and that is crucial to development. In a remote culture, you want to be able to optimize those qualities.

My huddle with a colleague in Singapore was in the evening in my time zone, but early the next morning for him. Creating a meeting space in this manner did not make the distance obvious, but made it disappear. It was a great way for me to end my day and for him to start his. We honored each other by making it work better for both of us to connect when the time was good in our geographical locations.

Most importantly, do not go into hibernation. Meet more often with shorter check-in times, just to connect. One way to make the distance disappear and to encourage engagement is to have stand-ups. Every person has two minutes to say what they are working on that week or what they accomplished the week before.

Another idea is to share in birthdays, anniversaries, and special events as a team to help grow the feeling of community. Depending on how diverse your team is, you can highlight the multicultural expertise of the team by creating times for members to share about their cultures or holidays and what they celebrate. All of these ideas make the geographical distance disappear while the team bonds and becomes more connected.

Culture Teams

My husband Rick's company has a combination workforce with many co-located at headquarters and just as many located out in the field—working from anywhere. To accommodate, they created Culture Teams. Like Laura's company, their idea was to develop engagement to make employees feel unified.

One of the activities they developed was a short "Happy Hour" time done over video conferencing towards the end of the day. These events are done once a month or every quarter, depending on how long the team has been together. The laughter and ribbing while sharing snacks and drinks was a unifying, yet relaxing atmosphere. For three to five minutes, one employee will do a "show and tell" style talk. One employee took everyone on a tour of their art studio, telling them about what they do outside of work, and shared some of their artwork. Another took the video outside and showed the team the landscaping that they had been working so hard on.

One of the most important things about remote teams is to build one that has connection and strength. When teams have the time and ability to bond with one another, it makes them stronger overall and a cohesive unit.

Christmas Gift Exchange

When I was a Global Director at Polycom, each year we had a remote Christmas/Holiday gift-exchange party for my team. Yep! You read that correctly! There were about twelve of us widespread across the world. From the U.S., to Australia, to the UK, to Singapore, this is one thing we loved to do every year. As we would celebrate, it became apparent how much we really knew about one another, even though we never worked in the same location.

Prior to the party, two team members met over VC and drew names for everyone. Then they sent emails to each of us individually to let us know whose name we had. We would buy a present and wrap it so that it was not obvious who sent it, or who had their name. I found ordering online with delivery became the most cost-effective way to send gifts especially with sending it internationally. An anonymous note was added which said, "Wait to open." When the gift came, we would put it under the tree and wait until our holiday party.

Our holiday exchange was set at a time convenient to the greatest majority of the team. During the party, we had holiday foods at each of our locations. Gathering by video, we would do fun things like wearing silly sweaters and then take turns opening our gifts in front of the group. It developed a deeper camaraderie among our team. One at a time each person opened their gift, and guessed who had their name.

Through the years, we looked forward to the party with great anticipation. Others in the company on cross-functional teams began to ask if they could join. It became a treasured tradition.

When you conduct business by video, you recreate an in-person experience. Body language cannot be seen unless you produce this face-to-face visual interaction. There is a deeper connection with your teammates, with customers, and with your experts. There is more flexibility overall that can lead to having a stronger presence, and ultimately leads to operational efficiency.

On Your Own

For those who work remotely as a freelancer or entrepreneur, feeling engaged and eliminating isolation is important as well. Work to connect with clients or collaborative partners. Use co-working hubs occasionally. You would be amazed how a video or phone call every few weeks with a former colleague or friend can boost your morale.

Final Thoughts on Engagement

Utilize socialization tools to deliberately develop relationships. Slack and HipChat are great options. Even LinkedIn and Facebook offer some level of engagement and connecting. Whenever possible, consider having on-site convergence every few years. If it is not feasible, use video conferencing to emulate it much more often.

Like Laura's and Rick's companies do, if you practice healthy engagement, you will have connected camaraderie and boost morale. Consider the culture of your remote workplace and what you are doing to make the distance disappear.

CHAPTER 3

Management of Self and Team

A dear friend of mine, Paul Bardack, and I served on the U.S. Distance Learning Association board of directors together for many years. In his role as an attorney, Paul was actually the person who President George H. W. Bush sent to California to handle arbitration during the Rodney King riots. Paul currently serves as the Executive Director of the Maryland Small Business Development Center. He works remotely and has an office at a WeWork co-working space that is affiliated with the University of Maryland College Park.

The entire bottom floor of the facility has collaborative workspaces designed for creativity, comfort, and productivity—with an espresso bar, of course. The second floor is glass-clad private offices, one of which he occupies several days a week. Startups, small businesses, and entrepreneurs share the two floors of this space.

Paul is a high-energy, extremely-social kind of guy who thrives in being around people. At his WeWork remote office, he finds the "life" springing forth from those sharing the space invigorating. Like me, Paul is at his peak of productivity and creativity early in the morning, before his day can be interrupted by others. As he puts it, "I get my day started before my personal rhythm is influenced by the rhythm of others and I become more reactive than proactive."

Paul not only manages himself, but has a large team of remote employees working from home and other locations across his state. He believes a leader of an organization is only as good as his people. If you ask him to describe his job in one sentence he would say, "My job is to identify the people in my organization who really want to deliver excellence, and to empower them to do it."

Paul does just that. His highly-engaged team feels valued and empowered under his leadership. While going remote adds flexibility and freedom, with it comes a new set of management challenges. As Paul demonstrates, it's vital to adapt and enable yourself and your team to do great work from anywhere.

You could be like Paul and manage teams spread across a large region. You could have a far-flung team with highly variant schedules. You could be a freelancer or entrepreneur that has to manage yourself and your client relationships. Regardless, in remote management there are challenges.

Challenges

Transitioning from working in a conventional office environment to working from anywhere takes organization and a little bit of control. Besides the challenge to adapt to a remote-work lifestyle where we stay engaged and motivated, the question then becomes: "How do you prevent or overcome the management challenges of planning, organizing, staffing, leading, and controlling?" It takes knowing the best way to work independently, and if leading a team(s), knowing the best way to manage others.

If it is not done well it can lead to long hours, tight deadlines, and an endless to-do list, which has become common in the modern workstyle and leads to nothing but burnout. Done well, the best results foster a confident, collaborative, and creative work culture with less stress and anxiety, and a healthy balance between professional and home life.

Defining and Managing Expectations

A successful remote employee can be fairly independent and knows how to do their job well. When you set up your remote office space, in essence you are setting boundaries both physically and mentally. You define a space and the idea of setting apart work from your personal life and establish somewhat of a schedule.

After that, it is a matter of managing your time and productivity. Define realistic expectations and guidelines that fit your situation. If your organization has been allowing employees to work remotely for a long time there is most likely a policy guidebook, ground rules, or expectations already in place.

For example, you need to determine how flexible and autonomous you can be with your time and schedule. This could be working hours as well as days worked. Are there organization expectations already defined? Are you expected to be "at your desk" for the traditional eight-hour-a-day, five-days-a-week work schedule, or is there more flexibility than that? Some organizations allow remote employees to set deadlines with the freedom to work when and where they want to work, as long as the work gets done. Flexible hours for some could mean flextime, a compressed workweek, shift work, or job-sharing.

Do you have guidelines and expectations in place that allow for healthy collaboration? Some use an app where people can communicate quickly and efficiently and can share their location and availability with the co-workers. There are other technologies out there that can be used similarly. You just need to find out what structure you want to use, and how to create that for your team.

Consider some of the subtle changes that will come as you begin to work remotely. When you get stuck on something or have a quick question, you can't glance across the office to see if Ron is sitting at his desk. If you work for a global company, you might be part of a team that is extremely geographically dispersed. Working together takes a unique approach. In fact, what hours you work could change daily. To communicate and work effectively takes a new tactic. Whether managing yourself or a team, you will be evolving some practices.

Time Management

Starting with healthy boundaries for personal-life and work-life separation is important. Determine what hours you will be available. Sometimes schedules collide. Perhaps you have a coworker in another part of the world who needs your support for a meeting that is late at night or early in the morning for you. It takes a bit of adjusting and flexibility.

While I worked at Polycom, oftentimes my global counterparts would need me in the middle of my night. I adjusted. On occasion, one of my children would have a program during school, or I would have a doctor's appointment. I adjusted.

Being flexible with my hours, I could easily adjust to meet any demands of my time. Quite often during the week, my hours were far from a set 8-5 workday, but I made sure I always worked beyond the total number of expected hours per week. It was a matter of finding a healthy balance between my work and personal life. Even with the flexibility I had to understand that there will be shorter work times and longer ones beyond normal work hours, but that they balance out. Creating general parameters gives you a baseline from which to start.

Another parameter that needs to be established, with regards to time management, is setting communication response time expectations. Determine how fast response times should be. While communication and constant knowledge-sharing is important for staying connected and engaged, the negative side is when others expect you to reply instantly. This can interrupt your workflow and concentration. I call these rhythm busters.

Trying to give quick replies and be helpful could eat up your entire day. As an individual or manager, establishing ground rules here will make life easier for everyone. Designate modes of communication based on activities, such as when to use video, email, or chat apps. Also set ground rules around which app to use based on urgency. Set rules that define response time expectations. Make sure they work for everyone— keeping in mind any time-zone variations.

I find that quick questions done by text can take less time than when I was in an office and people would stop by my desk to ask, as there is not as much chit-chat. Still it is important when managing your schedule to buffer for interruptions.

Set parameters for "going dark" or "heads down" when you will be in a "not to be disturbed" mode.

Determine how often you will go dark, and for what reasons. Certain tasks or projects that require your full attention need a do not disturb sign. Sometimes it is needed when you are in an important meeting.

Without being in the same location, people can't see that you are busy. Apps that let you set your status as "available," "unavailable," or "do not disturb" can make it easy for coworkers to know when not to interrupt. Establish an emergency backchannel for when it is absolutely necessary to interrupt someone.

With expectations set, you can get down to managing your schedule. Organization is crucial to accomplishing key tasks and tracking completion. From a management perspective, determining how to measure performance when working remotely takes a bit of adjustment.

Measuring Performance

One of the biggest concerns I hear from managers is that they don't know how to know for certain their remote employees are actually working. Just because remote workers are out of the office doesn't mean their work can't be tracked, managed, or documented. It is simply a matter of adjusting how you measure performance.

From a management perspective, something to consider is hours versus seat time. In our less-than-modern way, traditionally, we have always had a structured 8-hour workday that starts definitively at one time and ends definitively at another time. The expectation is that your rear should be in the chair the whole time, focused, with only a couple of breaks including lunch. Then you go home, and work is over.

When you work remotely, flexibility and autonomy tend to erase that environment. Unless you have billable hours or a specific job which requires it, measuring by seat time may also go away. Some people expect remote employees to keep that same structured schedule, even while working from home, so that everything is kept fair amongst their co-located counterparts in the organization. At that point, you measure productivity according to what you are accomplishing during an 8-hour day. However, there is a new system in place—a new matrix of measuring productivity—not by focusing on hours worked, but by focusing on benchmarks and targets met. Ultimately this leads to greater productivity overall, and contributes to greater retention, because each person is able to tailor the work to their personal rhythm, and not be overwhelmed with the workload.

Although you can easily track seat time through software, timesheets, or self-regulation, the remote employee's productivity can more appropriately be measured by outcomes. Many remote managers use the KPI (Key Performance Indicators) approach based on productivity rather than seat time.

There will be periods when work can be done in shorter times, but sometimes it will take longer. You can somewhat balance the workload to an 8-hour day or 40-hour work week. The questions should then become: Are the indicators showing us that the employee is performing at the expected level set? Are remote employees getting the job done? Are they meeting deadlines?

For Paul Bardack, micromanagement was not an answer. Paul got to know his employees' skills and workstyles. As the leader, he simply estimates time to accomplish tasks then gives them room to get it done. Workloads hover around the 40-hour week levels. Any deadlines missed are discussed. If an employee constantly fails to perform at the expected level, then a more intense face-to-face discussion takes place. When necessary, different parameters and expectations are set for that employee. It is important to not punish others who work remotely or to determine the future of your remote-work policy based on one "bad apple" (one employee being unproductive).

Performance and Assignment Tracking

Whether managing yourself or a team, it is important to find a system that works for you. Create tasks with measurable goals, keeping an estimated time for completion that is based on skills and experience, then measure the outcomes.

As a remote team manager, knowing your team is crucial. Being aware of each team member's strengths and passions enables you to assign tasks accordingly. We all have tasks we don't like to do but have no choice. What is not fun to me might be your favorite thing to do. Knowing your team well enough to assign tasks accordingly not only makes measuring performance easier, but it also makes for a much more enjoyable work environment and increased productivity for your employees.

At one point in my career, I managed a remote team that was geographically dispersed globally. Our remote team was highly engaged and collaborating regularly. Quite often our project completion depended upon many moving parts (tasks) being done in a timely manner.

I had three people on a sub-team; all worked remotely. Two team members could be given a general concept and a goal and would run with it. The third team member needed all of the details and a linear, sequential timeline (plan). Without it, she was uncomfortable and unable to work at maximum proficiency. The first two team members could be asked to present to a customer on the fly, but the third team member needed sufficient time to know every detail before she felt comfortable enough to present.

They had different workstyles and personalities. Each had its own value. As the manager, I had to learn to delegate assignments in a way that didn't make the first two feel bogged down and the third to not feel like she was being forced to rely on her instincts rather than logic or knowledge.

How specific do you need to be when delegating tasks? Do you or your team need strong creative direction? Does the person you are managing need very specific concrete instructions, or can you give them general instructions and let them run with it? How solid of a picture do you have to give? Who on your team is outstanding at being the keeper of the documents? Who is best at customer-facing interactions? Who is creative and thinks outside the box? Who has the best skills for each type of assignment?

Leveraging or managing a project correctly can be the difference between success and failure. Understanding the proficiencies of each remote team member makes it easier to prevent the distance from impeding progress.

Managing Progress

Whether you are on a team or if it is just you, someone needs to know where you are in a process. They need to know how things are progressing and where you are in fulfilling a commitment.

Remote working requires transparency. Communication is also crucial. Make sure you communicate what you are working on and where you are in the process. Updating your team members will keep you focused and drive progress. How are you checking in with your team, your direct reports, and your stakeholders? A quick Internet search will reveal a ton of free and paid software tools for project management.

For remote team managers, have regular one-on-ones (1:1) with each team member as well as team calls. Make sure they have the resources and support needed. Ask them to share weekly highlights and lowlights and let you know of any barriers in their way. You will get a better feel of what you need to be doing.

People can queue up their questions for the 1:1 time. Rather than always interrupting your progress with questions that could wait, huddles can be a set time to ask and address needs. Video conferences are one of the best ways to huddle. Not only can you take a few moments to build camaraderie, but you can also get down to business and have a meeting of the minds. If you manage others who work remotely, you could have a far-flung team with highly variant schedules, so having huddles could take some thought when it comes to time zones.

Time-Zone Tracking and Courtesy

You can still meet and collaborate regularly even if your team is geographically dispersed around the world. If one member is in Singapore or Japan and the other is in America, making you at opposite ends of a day, meeting outside of normal business hours will be required for one of you. Across some countries, time zones change by 30 or 45 minutes rather than by an hour, so keeping up with the time differences to set meetings can be brutal. Tools like Every Time Zone can help you keep track.

Managing a team might mean setting deadlines for "End of Day" (EOD) rather than "Close of Business" (COB). Flexibility and clear communication on when and how to meet, as well as when deadlines are set takes some creativity. Whose day are you referring to when you set a deadline or meeting? It is important to not always make the same person sacrifice to meet late into the night or their early morning. Take turns or compensate those who sacrifice.

One person I managed ran our efforts in the Australian territory. We were fifteen hours apart by time zones. We would honor each other by trying to make our 1:1 huddle time in my late afternoon to early evening, which was her early morning the next day. Another team member was based in London, six hours ahead of me so we learned to use the variance of time zones to our advantage.

Sometimes I would drive collaborative efforts by dividing projects where a team member from each region of the world managed tasks during their day and could pass it off to the next team member who was just starting their day. They could keep the focus running with that project while the other team members slept. In some cases, my team members shifted their hours to huddle together as desired. The flexibility of remote work allowed each person to manage their own productivity time. As an added benefit, it also gave our organization 24/7 coverage.

When Dr. Susan Aldridge was at University of Maryland University College (UMUC), she used an international team with TATA Group to design simulations for high-end cybersecurity courses. At the end of the day in the US, the project was handed off to the team in India. At the end of their day, it was handed back to the US team. This was an extremely labor-intensive project but due to the multiple time zones, it was literally completed in half the time. This requires an extremely detailed work plan.

Making time zones work for you is a great way to get work done continuously and promote productivity. When one person can pass off the project at night to a person who is just rising for the day, work continues on the project. The flexibility of allowing others to work during times that work best for them makes the distance disappear and works to your advantage in completing projects.

Finally

Yes indeed, going remote adds flexibility and freedom that comes with a new set of management challenges.

Like Paul Bardack does, when managing yourself or others, it is vital to adapt and enable yourself and your team to do great work from anywhere. By taking a step back, prioritizing and taking control, you can foster a confident, collaborative, and creative work culture while maximizing productivity.

CHAPTER 4

Operating at a High Level of Productivity

Over the last few weeks, my family has been developing a vegetable garden area. We created the space and prepared the soil with organic additives. My son built a really nice irrigation system, but unfortunately got a bad case of poison ivy in the process. My husband and daughter researched and selected which vegetables they wanted to grow, since they do most of the cooking. My daughter-in-law created a spreadsheet to better educate us on each type of plant.

With the garden prepared, we planted seeds, some directly in the garden and some in sprouting containers. We taught our younger grandkids how important it is to know the best season for each type of vegetable, as well as how far apart to space the seeds, and the depth to plant them. We all learned how to care for the garden so that it yields the best crop. The entire family, young and old, played a role.

It doesn't work to just throw a bunch of seeds and hope they produce. The same is true when working remotely. You can't just throw a bunch of tasks at yourself or someone else and hope to produce good results.

Challenges

While gardening is fun, it can also be very challenging. There is a subtle art and science, since many plants require delicately-balanced conditions in order to thrive. Operating at a high level of performance is an art, but like gardening, it comes with challenges to maintain balanced conditions.

Whether we like it or not, working remotely has the inaccurate stigma that makes some people wonder what remote workers do all day. It leads them to imagine we are not working at the level of an 8-hour day.

On the other hand, dealing with the challenging expectation that you should be available outside of normal business hours and always working is not fun. In reality, without going to an office and being able to leave work behind each day, things can quickly get out of control. You don't stop to eat. You work late into the night or on weekends. This can lead to insomnia. No time spent refreshing or reenergizing puts your brain in overdrive and leads to burnout with impaired productivity.

Regardless of either scenario, what we accomplish or produce is the only evidence of our labor. To produce and yield the best results possible will take a planned approach with skillful execution. Done right, you can enjoy an excellent harvest while keeping your workload under control so that you do not become overwhelmed.

Foundation and Preparation

Remote work, just like with gardening, starts with a good foundation and the right preparation. Success depends upon choosing a great location, defining the layout, getting the right tools, and preparing the soil.

Productivity is a measure of efficiency. Just like an efficient garden reaps a great harvest, an efficient system will enable you to operate at a high level of productivity. If you have already defined your remote workspace, then you have picked the optimal location where you can be the most productive. An engaging remote environment, the right tools (technologies), finding your rhythm, and practicing good management skills will give you a well-prepared start.

If the foundation of a garden, the soil, is not healthy, you cannot expect much from your plants. Working the soil is like developing your to-do list for maximum productivity. The general productivity rules that apply no matter what your work environment is, apply here. As you cultivate the soil, which is, in this case, your to-do list, you give yourself a healthy start as you plan your week, your day.

Crushing Your To-Do List

Regardless of where you work, high-level performance starts with cultivating basic productivity habits to help you maximize your efficiency. Once these are in order, you can crank away at crushing your to-do list.

To focus on what is important and cultivate deep work, we must begin with organizing a list of tasks, assignments, projects, etc. A to-do list with realistic hours to complete each project should also identify the importance of each task: high, medium, or low priority. In other words, determine what is the most urgent, what is important, and what can wait. When appropriate, share the list with your boss to determine the order of importance.

Most often, working remotely not only offers flexibility, but also allows you to take care of other pressing things, in addition to your work obligations. The best practices are to find what works for you, as you organize commitments, prioritize your day, and establish good habits.

Determine who needs to be involved because you have to get on their calendars. Working remotely— especially if you and your team are in different time zones—can slow down progress or bring productivity to a halt if scheduling cross-collaboration has not been taken into account.

When you need support from someone to get past the problem, you could impede progress if they are not available. There is nothing worse than someone expecting you to drop everything so you can complete something on their to-do-lists that needs your support. Even when requesting support from someone else for something small, give them plenty of time to add it into their calendar.

As I write this, I received a text asking me to create a 20-second video to say hi to my students. I don't mind doing that, but the deadline was in 4 hours. Seems simple enough, however, it interrupted my focus, plus, it meant I had to actually get dressed (at least from the waist up) and put on makeup. Ugh! Another advantage/disadvantage to working remotely.

Based on your rhythm, the hours you work each day, and your priorities, as well as knowing the best times that work for your co-workers who are supporting or working with you, decide what can be accomplished in one day. Keep high-priority and brain-taxing items scheduled for your peak performance hours and when you will least likely be interrupted. So much more can be accomplished with mental sharpness.

Of course, it is important to practice good time-management skills to maximize concentration and decrease distraction. Breaking tasks into smaller pieces and batching your activities into dedicated time blocks enables you to streamline completion. Practice "calendar chunking" based on estimated completion times for tasks and chunk them into manageable sizes.

Remember, your manager can't see how many hours you are putting in and how focused you are. Quite often projects or assignments require longer hours and more intense focus that we generally think. Something that seems like a walk in the park to them often takes more problem solving than expected. Unless you communicate this, your manager is unaware of unknown "gotchas."

Get Going

A great way to get going is by putting first things first, as Steven Covey wrote in *7 Habits of Highly Effective People*. He advocated focusing on the most important tasks first. Others suggest you do the biggest or least-preferred activity first to get it out of the way.

Mark Twain once said, "If it's your job to eat a frog, it's best to do it first thing in the morning. And if it's your job to eat two frogs, it's best to eat the biggest one first." The key is to follow your planned schedule, while allowing it to be flexible and adaptable as needed. Plan for things to possibly go wrong and for unexpected glitches. Make sure you eliminate inefficient communications.

A former colleague of mine had an excellent system that worked for her. Working remotely meant very little time in the office, and for her to be out-and-about most of the day. She had the good habit of ending her workday by recapping what had been accomplished, what was left undone, and any new items that need to be added to her to-do list. Then, she could schedule what she needed to accomplish the next day.

What works best for me is using the Uncalendar or something similar to keep everything I am working on organized. I like having sections for itemizing each task on my list, as well as having areas to group tasks by project. In another section, I can include my personal commitments and to-do lists. With the ability to quickly organize what I want to accomplish for the day, I am able to easily log progress on every aspect.

At a glance, I ask myself what one thing has to be done today. What are two or three other important things that need to be worked on or completed? And, I look at what I need to do at home which I don't want to get distracted by during work hours.

Unless I have plans to start my day focused on a huge project, I like to schedule a meeting for first thing in the morning. Working remotely takes discipline to get up and moving when the office is just down the hall and you don't have to necessarily get dressed. A meeting is one way to get me up and going early. Otherwise, I schedule according to my personal rhythm.

When my son was in the U.S. Air Force Presidential Honor Guard, one of his favorite sayings was "Move with a purpose." That statement works for all of us when it comes to operating at a high level of productivity. We should all move with a purpose.

Purposeful Focus vs. Distractions

To cultivate deep work requires removing any distractions and having purposeful focus. Interruptions throw you off balance. Every time you lose focus by doing something else, it can take several minutes to get back to where you were. The more interruptions, the more time is being wasted. In a remote environment, distractions occur just as they do when co-located, however, it is a different set. To move with a purpose and have purposeful focus requires controlling distractions.

Consider how weeds and pests are detrimental to your garden. You can save plants from being devoured by unwanted creatures by placing flowering ones like marigolds on the parameter. The flowers attract and feed all of the insects you don't want devouring your crops, which saves your vegetables.

What are the weeds and pests in your remote office? The distractions? Is it constantly responding to texts or emails? Is it answering a need of someone in the house? Is it all of the chaos going on around the house or chores calling your name?

While finding our rhythm and determining purposeful periods of focus is extremely valuable, so is learning to manage interruptions and distractions effectively. We have to get control of the weeds and the pests. Whether you are working remotely or working co-located, the interruption can be the same, such as focusing too much on administrative tasks or from co-workers needing your attention. However, when working remotely, interrupting co-workers cannot see how deeply focused you are, so they cannot gauge when to approach you.

One remote worker got extremely frustrated by a colleague who always demanded her time. The co-worker regularly wanted her to stop everything she was doing and to focus on helping him get an assignment completed which required her support. When she began to push back on the interruptions by offering to schedule him into her calendar at a time that worked for her, he reported her to her manager as slacking off and not being willing to help. This gentleman was a dedicated worker, a good man, but didn't know what she was working on, nor how hard she was working. He assumed she had all of time in the world and since the assignment included her, it should be at the top of her priority list. He had no idea how his constant interruptions were preventing her from crushing her own to-do list.

When remote, understand that others—just like you—work hard and need to control interruptions. They have to manage their own weeds and pests. Let your manager and team members know what you are working on. For a longer task, such as one that will take you three hours to complete, some remote workers prefer to schedule it first and then set a timer to go off after three hours. Others go dark with strong "do not disturb" signs on the perimeter of their office. Others move with a purpose by keeping administrative tasks in one place to weed through at a set time on their calendars. When necessary, use technology to show you have "gone dark" for purposeful focus. Find a healthy balance between helping others and getting your own to-do list done.

When moving with a purpose, we should not allow distractions to get in the way of reaching a goal. Be considerate of others and plan accordingly so that you aren't a negative interruption to them.

What are your marigolds? What do you do to stop pests from interrupting your rhythm? What weeds threaten to take over your remote workspace? How creative can you be in managing interruptions and distractions?

One radical idea about eliminating distractions came from a new division president I had at AT&T. To put it into perspective, when you have 300,000 employees in a company, I would approximate that a division was 30,000 to 50,000 people. Our president made a rule that there was to be no emails on Wednesdays. The uproar from the employees was almost audible from everywhere in the country.

At first, we thought he was completely nuts. He made it clear that they were watching emails and reiterated that no one could write or respond to any emails on Wednesdays. It was only a matter of a few weeks, however, before people started saying that they got more accomplished on Wednesdays than they did the rest of the week! We were shocked. Not only were the employees happier because they were getting things accomplished, the speed of productivity increased and satisfied customers abounded.

A no-email policy might not work for everyone, but perhaps a no-scheduled-meetings policy for a day might! Determine what works best for you. Perhaps it could be a "going dark" day with limited interruptions to include email and meetings.

Intentional Interruptions

Distractions, like weeds and pests, can stop or decrease productivity. But not all interruptions need to be unwanted distractions. Productivity can also decrease because we lose focus as we get tired. Like fertilizing plants in a garden, people need to be re-energized. Interrupting ourselves to re-energize can help us get going again. While focusing on your target projects is imperative, I and many others find it useful to schedule in interruptions. Intentionally.

Take care of your mind and body. Take a break to re-energize. Refresh your brain. Manage your energy and your time. Like plants need the night to rejuvenate, you too need your rest. If you expect the garden to produce, you'll have to water and fertilize regularly. Providing these necessities throughout the growing season helps plants grow fast, establish strong roots, and produce the most fruit.

The same is true if you want maximum productivity for yourself. To produce at a higher level requires a time of rest, nourishing, and refreshing. When you have been working non-stop with purposeful focus and have completed an assignment or section of it, take a refreshing break. I call these "intentional interruptions."

Another advantage of working from home or anywhere is that it makes for treasured breaks. An intentional interruption might be to get something done in your personal life which gives you a sense of accomplishment. It could be a chore, stopping to spend time with a loved one, or taking a walk. Even a short power nap can reinvigorate you.

When I accomplish something from my list, I take a scheduled break. If I need to stretch or clear my head to regain focus, I take an intentional interruption. It re-energizes me to play with the kids, pet the dog, or grab delivered packages off of the porch.

When I finish a task fifteen minutes early, I take five minutes to recap what was discussed, outline the next steps, and notate who is responsible. I then spend ten minutes for an intentional interruption. There is nothing like a good hug to get rejuvenated or inspired. A clear mind helps you focus again. Choosing to have purposeful focus with intentional interruptions is a powerful way to maximize productivity.

Balancing Time

While water is refreshing, too much or not enough water can be detrimental to a garden. Just like too many distractions can result in reducing productivity, so can lacking breaks. There must be a time to disconnect; to know when to stop for the much-needed long period of rest and not just take an intentional interruption.

Set a start and finish line. Clear your mind at the end of the workday and adjust your schedule for the next day. It is important to be real with yourself and understand that the work will never be completely done. It will still be there tomorrow. And unless there is a solid deadline that is critical, then setting a specific time for the end of the workday is a good way to ensure you keep a good balance of your time. It takes self-discipline to stop to achieve the best work/life balance.

High-Powered Prioritization

Many companies are piling all the work on one person and reducing their staffing. We could work 365/24-7 and we would never get it all done. This is the moment when you need to recognize this calls for "high-powered prioritization."

How do you prioritize when everything is a high-level priority? When everything needs done now, how do you manage the pressure and intensity? High-powered prioritization is to ambitiously arrange everything that needs to be accomplished so you can gain control for a healthy work/life balance.

Hopefully, you have already determined how long it will take to complete each task, and with that allowed a time cushion for any unexpected challenges. If you are like me, I tend to underestimate how long it will take for me to get something done. My husband always overestimates. The best scenario is to be able to finish on-time or early, so I adjust my calculations accordingly. Logically consider what you can get done in a few hours, one day, or longer. Be honest with yourself about the time commitment, and take care of yourself.

When you use high-powered prioritization, you have to make tough decisions since more than likely you cannot do it all. You determine where you think it is most important to spend your purposeful, focused time. Look at any smaller items you can tackle in your less-than-peak-performance brain time. Oftentimes our managers will say, "It all is important," but is that realistic? If it is simply impossible to meet all of the deadlines, have a discussion with your leader(s) to visibly lay it all out. Together you can figure out what is most important to accomplish.

Similar to the way that pruning results in a healthier, more vigorous plant, pruning your to-do list by practicing high-powered prioritization, having manageable expectations and a healthy balance results in high-level productivity and better outcomes.

Deadheading and Sufficient Excellence

Another way to improve the results in a garden is by removing spent flowers. Called deadheading, this process encourages plants to place energies into stronger leaves and roots and gives room for new blooms. Despite the ominous sound, deadheading is nothing more than trimming off spent flowers, keeping plants tidy, and ensuring maximum bloom time.

A good practice of deadheading should be done as you work through your prioritized list. Trim and tidy up in a way that removes dead weight and encourages you to produce better. Your work needs room to bloom to reach its full potential.

- Do you ever find yourself in the middle of a project that you keep trying to make perfect, but you get bogged down in the weeds or end up focusing on something that has passed its usefulness?

- Have you focused energy on things that no longer need your attention?

- Have you been caught up in doing something a certain way because that is the way it has always been done?

- Have you spent countless hours working through a process that is outdated or unnecessary, leaving you with no energy left to streamline a project?

Deadheading will help you tidy up and trim away debris and items that are no longer useful so you can meet a deadline. If necessary, use your remote team when you are unsure if something is spent and ready to trim. If you are working collaboratively on a project, remote team huddles play an important role. What might look spent to you might be less obvious to someone else.

One manager spent countless hours trying to get his less-successful employees to change their bad habits. Finally, he created a success plan, outlining agreed-upon gaps and what steps needed to be taken to close those gaps. Then, taking one step at a time, he would meet with each employee weekly to help them make progress. He gave them a clear path for success.

For most of these employees, the process worked, and they were grateful for the coaching and outcomes. For some it did not work. They could not make the necessary changes, which led to them being let go. The manager, in essence, practiced deadheading in two ways. Firstly, he saved himself from spending countless hours with little success by changing the process. Secondly, he removed unproductive employees which made room for new employees to bloom.

While deadheading is important, knowing when to harvest is also crucial. When a garden begins to produce, it must be harvested promptly. Vegetables left in the garden too long will rot. Know when to deadhead and when to harvest. Pay attention to when a project is done to satisfaction and ready to harvest. I call it "sufficient excellence."

In striving for excellence—particularly if you are a perfectionist—fewer outcomes are produced because more time is spent on making something more perfect than necessary. Doing the work of three people means more output is required from you, and the idea of perfect can get in the way.

Likewise, we can be so creative and innovative that we keep working and reworking a project or assignment to the point where we become bogged down. Being overly perfect eats up your time. When something is "perfect," oftentimes it is based on our opinion, but shouldn't it be the bosses' or customer's? Who is the task or project being done for? We should always strive for excellence, but where do you draw the line?

Being sufficient, rather than overly perfect, gets the job done. It might well be ready for harvest, and good enough to get off of our plate so we can move on to the next project. This is where sufficient excellence comes into play.

This does not mean that you cannot go back later and tweak or rework something. The entire point of sufficient excellence is to ask yourself who you are serving. Is it excellent to them? It does not necessarily need to measure up to your "perfection" standards or to your highest level of creativity. If others think it is awesome, then you have achieved what you set out to achieve.

Knowing if what you are working on is sufficiently excellent sometimes can be hard, especially when you are remote. You might want to hop on a video call with a colleague or your manager for a quick review. Along the way, it helps to bounce ideas off of others to best determine if something is fully ripe.

By practicing sufficient excellence to get each task done adequately, you can move on to the next task and increase the quantity of what you are producing. Sufficient excellence allows you to crush your to-do list and ensures maximum productivity.

Finally

Gardening can be overwhelming at times, however, it is work with a hefty reward. You get tons of fresh vegetables, herbs, and fruit. You also know where they came from and what went into them, giving you the peace of mind that you are not ingesting unwanted, harmful chemicals. It is also a great way to get outside and enjoy the fresh air. The joy of working remotely brings an even more hefty reward when you operate with a high level of productivity, and revolutionize the way things get done.

CHAPTER 5

Trust & Team

One of my family's favorite pastimes is watching reruns of the "The Joy of Painting." Bob Ross achieved pop-culture fame in the 1980s as the bushy-haired public television host. Millions of viewers worldwide continue to enjoy the show today. It is easy to become quickly enamored with his calming voice and positive messages, but it is the way he makes painting seem so easy that astonishes many.

While making it look incredibly easy so you can replicate the skill at home, he walks viewers through the "wet-on-wet" oil painting method, step-by-step on each of his compositions. Bob painted breathtaking landscapes beginning with backgrounds such as mountains or a forest, then added rocks, grass, water sources, and trees in the foreground, and eventually birds in the sky.

To produce a beautiful work of art like those Bob Ross created, requires a well-orchestrated design composition. The word "composition" comes from the Latin word componere, meaning "put together." Keeping fundamental principles of design, Bob put together a composition by placing visual elements on canvas.

The design "building blocks" of a composition include balance, unity, harmony, alignment, repetition, and emphasis. Following the principles of design composition not only make a piece of art eye-catching and dynamic, but it evokes a response from the viewer. You can recognize a great artist by how their work makes others feel.

How well-designed is your remote culture? How does your company make people feel? Externally? Internally? What is the composition of your company? Your teams? Is there trust? Do you work well together?

Remote work, done wrong, can throw a company off-balance and lead to mistrust, conflict, and a lack of unity or harmony. Remote work, done right, will produce a masterpiece that resonates with your customers and employees, builds trust, and makes them feel confident knowing you care.

The Power of Trust

Trust must flow throughout an organization regardless of where people are located. Have you ever felt apprehensive about trusting a colleague? Did you wonder if they look out for your best interests or only their own? Have you had concern in trusting that your colleague is capable and reliable?

Being at a distance makes trusting even more difficult. You can't physically observe your co-workers or leadership. Having strong relational and competence-based trust are foundational principles of any organization's success, but especially in designing a healthy remote-culture composition.

When a company decides to enable remote work, a major focus should be to make sure there is a solid foundation of trust. Creating a healthy remote culture, with trust at its core, is the most powerful way to not only enable high performance across an organization, but to be the best company you can be, so the world can see what you are made of.

A culture of trust begins with authenticity, integrity, kindness, and good humor—where everyone feels valued. It fosters a strong rapport with the belief that we are all in this together. Whether top down, bottom up, or sideways, trust should become part of the DNA of the company, along with the vision and core values. With a unified approach and the ability to take ownership of everything that is done, comes the greatest success.

Unilaterally, a healthy remote team is a connected community built on trust. Just as visual elements in a painting work together, trust and the true meaning of team underlie a great composition. To create a beautiful work of art (product) requires a strong foundation of trust, with key elements working harmoniously, layer upon layer, in order to be most effective.

Of course, there must be mutual accountability between supervisors and employees. Regardless of your role, feedback to let someone know what can be done to improve performance is extremely important—especially for remote workers. Likewise, the metrics showing accountability can validate success.

The Bob Ross Approach

Bob Ross could make paintings that were realistic in nature and beautiful to look at, and it didn't even take him a week to finish just one. He filmed one entire season of his PBS show in just two days. Much of the work was done beforehand.

Bob created three paintings for every episode he did. The first one was his prototype and sat off camera as a reference. The second one he did live on air. For Bob's "How To" books, the third rendition was done with a photographer looking over his shoulder to take snapshots of each step along the way. Bob knew where he was going when he was on camera. He had planned it all ahead of time and had already done it. Each episode was the result of his investment of time and effort.

Ultimately, organizations want the customer to see the care given to providing them with a solution to their problem. Does the solution meet their challenges? We want to create solutions that are a masterpiece. A perfect trifecta requires three principle design elements: a solid foundation of core values/vision, a strong team, and brilliant execution. It's all about the outcomes. I call this the "Bob Ross Approach."

Give Background

Start by painting the background and building from there. People want to work for a company that has set the right course and a culture where employees can feel safe and know the direction the company is headed.

With the Bob Ross Approach, the painted background is the vision casting. Like Bob, who was able to see his vision and walk viewers through the process even though they were at a distance, remote workers need a clear picture of the core values, the mission, and the purpose. With the vision ingrained in each individual's DNA, as part of who they are, employees can take ownership in confidence.

As a remote employee, more than ever we need to know how we contribute overall to the goals as an individual, as a team, and as a cross-team. Having everyone on the same page and speaking the same language builds trust, unity, and connectedness.

Do remote employees have any idea of what's going on at headquarters (HQ)? For the remote employee, not being a part of a meeting at HQ where the vision is cast can be a critical mistake. Employees need to be aware of special business in the company, beyond just the vision, such as organizational realignment, promotions, people leaving, mergers/acquisitions, etc.

There are advantages to being out of the day-to-day office politics, but not being aware of things going on that ultimately impact an employee can be very frustrating. It is important to make remote employees feel as if they aren't missing out on anything. Making meetings of importance live and virtually accessible is crucial.

Know Your Team

Another element of the Bob Ross Approach is knowing your composition. How well do you know your team? Do you know their skills and competencies? Their preferences? What type of people compose your team?

You have to know composition in order to execute the vision of what you first pictured in your mind. Bob Ross would add some trees in the foreground to change the composition as needed. Sometimes he would say, "Every tree needs a little friend," and then add another tree to the image. By grouping trees, Bob would strike a great balance on canvas.

The woods across the lake from my back-porch office are made of a variety of trees such as maple, oak, three varieties of pine, and dogwood. The panorama creates a beautiful display of color and textures blending together to bring a sense of tranquility to the end of a long workday. The scenery is heightened by the stunning reflection across the water, and each season has its own showcase of splendor. It reminds me of my remote team that I mentioned earlier.

Our team was a diverse, multicultural group geographically dispersed worldwide—people with different backgrounds, cultures, and experiences; each of us bringing our own texture and color, so to speak. We were a close team because we knew each other well. We learned about each other's various cultures, holidays, and practices, in addition to knowing strengths, personalities, and workstyles. Having a deep level of understanding not only built trust, but also empowered us to flourish independently and collaboratively as a team. Our high-performance level not only served our organization, it reflected well for the company image. The team struck a great balance in our composition.

Consider each tree as a member of the remote team. Sometimes, the work an individual does is designed to stand on its own. Other times, it is advantageous to compose a team of people to complete a project. Knowing personalities of the team players and the differences in workstyles is crucial for the best composition. Teamwork and infrastructure are very important to a remote culture. More and more often today, virtual collaboration is critical in business. It is the new normal. Invest in knowing your team.

Deliberate investment to know your team well can be the difference between success and failure. It allows you to build optimal teams and develop trust. When you work remotely, you've got to be purposeful about developing those relationships. If you are not co-located, you cannot just stop by someone's office and have a chat. Some special thought needs to be put into building healthy work-relationships across teams. Working remotely means connecting on purpose.

A deep trust will come when each person is invested in one another's success. When you know the gifting and passions of each team member, no matter what position you hold, you will know who to call on for support. When they know you in the same manner, they will return the favor.

You should know the intent and heart of others. Someone on the team might be struggling. Unified teammates don't say, "Too bad," they chip in and help get things done, or they offer to coach them. Before focusing on execution, encourage a strong bond by developing the group.

The best composition of a remote team comes by recognizing the differences in personalities, cultures, giftings, and workstyles. Be a student of those you manage and serve. Study them enough to know their goals, listen intently, and learn. If you are a manager, compose teams based on skill sets or competencies paired with passions, and when appropriate, by time zones.

Know Your Cross Team

In addition to weekly small-team huddles and the time spent moving obstacles or coaching, a highly-successful remote manager named Rick deliberately invests his time with the cross teams. At least every quarter, he has one-on-one time with each of the members of his larger team. Cross-teams are the teams that interact with yours but are from different departments within the organization.

In Rick's company, individuals from different departments work together as cross-teams to manage specific clients. Rick understands the importance of not only knowing his team well, but also in getting to know his cross-team members too, in order to be most effective and productive in representing each client.

Through individual huddles with each cross-team member, Rick learns about their passions and giftings. He also understands how they are compensated, what their goals are, what they are tasked with doing, and how they work towards success.

Rick even knows their aspirations for their career path too. Sometimes he mentors or coaches them. Sometimes he just opens doors of opportunity for them in their career.

Many of the people he meets with work remotely, which makes Rick keenly aware of how difficult it might be for them to "get noticed" by other teams within his company. He shares with other leaders and managers across the country when he thinks one of his cross-team members may be a good fit in any new positions. He shares stories of his experience working with others and what he learns about each person so they can have a seat at the table when an opportunity comes along.

Rick has developed a reputation as a trusted leader and someone who helps others succeed. Without deliberately intending to, the trust and respect Rick has gained among them has resulted in anything he asks being expeditiously done. It has become a win for him and his team too.

If people care about one another, imagine what can be accomplished. If you honor one another, you will have a strong team bond and a culture of trust.

It is important to build relationships with individuals from both your team and your cross-team, and by building relationships with both teams as a larger group, you will deliver great returns on your investment.

Implementation

The final element of the Bob Ross Approach is execution or implementation. You have painted the picture, now it is time to do the work. Bob knew where he was going when he was on camera. He had planned it all and had already done it at least once. He knew what worked and didn't work before he implemented it on camera. He was well-prepared before painting in front of his customer, the viewer.

How do you do this when remote? Prepare before execution. With the background in place, and a well-defined foreground of team members each playing their role in the composition, the culture of trust will foster a "well-oiled" flow of implementation.

For remote salespeople, for example, preparing up front before you see customers will produce more opportunities and shorten the sales cycle. What seems easy and smooth took much preparation. Once preparation is completed, use the knowledge, the background, and groundwork for best implementation across your remote team.

While leveraging time zones works well for faster execution, it is equally important to honor teammates by respecting their personal time commitments. If they have a set time to pick up or drop off kids at school, honor that by not scheduling meetings at those times. Honor them by respecting their work/life balance and time. This shows respect and builds trust and team cohesiveness.

The flexibility of remote work allows each person to manage their own productivity time. Empower your remote team to handle anything that comes their way and to enjoy the autonomy and flexibility that comes from working remotely.

Perhaps most known for his "happy little accidents," Bob Ross would take a mistake and turn it into something even more beautiful than before. He did not allow setbacks to stop the process or cause any type of frustration. He would change the scene just a bit, or he would paint over the mistake to create something new.

The point he is making is that there is not a mess, and there are no mistakes. It is merely an opportunity to create a new solution. This is essential in creating resilience and agility within the team. Remote workers need to know how to take a setback and turn it into a positive that will eventually pay off. A culture of trust creates an environment of empowerment and innovation.

Finally

A healthy remote team does not allow the distance to drive wedges across their connected community, but uses it to best serve their customers. Creating a culture of trust not only serves your customers with the highest level of quality, it also leads to retaining all of your best employees.

Building on trust and team in the remote environment uses flexibility and autonomy to give remote employees a healthy work/life balance. Greater job satisfaction equals greater retention and less attrition.

German painter, William (Bill) Alexander had the original television series that inspired Bob Ross. Bill was a mentor to Bob and ultimately asked him to be his successor. Ross told viewers, "I feel as though he gave me a precious gift, and I'd like to share that gift with you." Isn't this what you hope others will say of you, your teammates, and ultimately your organization? A culture of trust makes working remotely a precious gift.

CHAPTER 6

Excellence

A few years back, my husband and I had our first experience participating in a regatta, which is a series of boat races. It was a company event. Two-time America's Cup Champion sailor and ESPN broadcaster, Peter Isler, was brought in to deliver a keynote address. In the breath-taking waters of the Santa Monica Bay against an azure sky sprinkled with puffs of clouds, the regatta followed.

Rick and I were extremely blessed to be placed on the six-person team assigned to a schooner with Peter Isler as the team coach! With very limited experience, the two of us were apprehensive yet excited, and as the only woman on board, I was even more so. For heaven's sake, Rick's CEO was part of our team. But true to his nature and giftedness, Peter taught each of us what we needed to know to perform.

The teams of the regatta were made up of company employees, fifteen or so sailboats in all. At the turning point of the race sat a larger vessel full of the employees who chose to observe rather than participate. Peter's

77

assistant was on board to narrate the event explaining what was happening and what to expect.

Because we had Peter on our boat for the first race, we gave a 10-minute head start to the other vessels—to make it fair, of course. We observed the other teams for a bit and waited for the fickle winds to provide us the best moment to kick into gear. Finally, the moment came to sail. We passed several teams with ease, but then came the turning point ahead. We could see two other schooners having trouble navigating the 90-degree turn to head back to where the race began. They appeared to be stalled, frantically trying to not collide with each other, as those on the observing vessel watched the chaos unfold in front of them. Just then, the winds picked up and our schooner started flying, dancing across the white crested waves, driving a path through the wind-whipped water—we were headed straight for them.

At the speed we were going, we were very concerned, but Peter's voice rang out telling each of us to be heads down and listen for his specific commands requiring our individual tasks. With my head down and focused, I heard a couple of the men offer to take over for me. Peter replied, "She can handle this. You do your job." Then, he commanded me to tack, which turns the bow toward the wind.

As we entered the area around the turning point—flying at full speed—each of us followed Peter's directions. We curved just inside the other vessels, within 15-20 feet of the other boats, and rounded the turning point to head back the way we came. This all happened in just a matter of seconds. Those on the observation deck of the large vessel were as flabbergasted as I was. It looked like calamity was about to happen, and yet our team acted with high-performance and extreme precision thanks to our team leader. With the captain at the helm, Peter was able to focus on coaching us to success. We became a team of excellence at the pinnacle of the sport and won the race.

Working remotely needs a team culture just like this, one that nurtures thriving productivity and fosters excellence; a confident, collaborative, and creative work environment. Just as Peter was able to build a high-performance team out of a group of people with greatly varied backgrounds (some with limited to no experience), it took desire on his part, as well as each team member, in order to succeed. Striving for excellence is a key principle of success for those working remotely.

Striving for Excellence

If organizations judge performance by the levels to which you meet expectations, then exceeding expectations or striving for excellence is our goal in order to reach the highest level of performance. It is the dream of human resources (HR) practitioners for employees to achieve excellence in the workplace. As individuals it should be our personal dream for ourselves—to be our best, to give our best.

When working remotely, whether for an organization or on your own, you will be known by the level of excellence you achieve. People come to know what they can expect from you. Those who work remotely are often concerned about having the opportunity to move up in an organization. So, how do you get noticed when you are not located with others? How do you prove yourself to others?

Recognition when working remotely necessitates striving for excellence. Be the kind of person who volunteers. Be of support to others. Be the kind of person your boss can learn from. You won't be invisible, nor feel isolated, but will have a sense of belonging, and more importantly, you will be a contributor. Strive to be an indispensable partner. Become a "known commodity" by always pushing yourself towards excellence. Always work to stretch and improve yourself.

Known Commodity

Paige and I were having lunch at a quaint diner in Seattle when the topic of her career came up. We discussed her aspirations and goals. Paige is someone who always strives for excellence in everything she does. She does her job with the goal to best serve others and the company. She seeks to stretch herself and to understand all perspectives of each person's role and goals.

Paige is driven to learn other areas of the company's business endeavors, and how the company's vision and goals are being met. In the first six months of employment, she discovered a process that was costing the company millions of dollars in revenue loss annually. She brought it to the company's attention, and showed how it could be fixed. She quickly became a known commodity.

Being the first to put up her hand to volunteer— even if it meant more hours for her—has enabled Paige to demonstrate striving for excellence. It helps her grow, innovate, and allows her to help others reach their goals. Having an attitude of excellence has taken her from starting at an entry level position, to leading a team. She became a liaison between two larger teams because of her knowledge and understanding of each team's processes and how they work.

Over lunch, Paige was sharing with me about a project in the area of "privacy" for which she had volunteered. She told me how fascinating she found the work to be, and that she dreamed of someday becoming a director of privacy.

Her phone rang and she excused herself saying it was the lead person on the project, so she needed to take the call. She thought it would only be a few minutes because they were wrapping up the project and he probably needed clarification.

Forty-five minutes later, she came back with a look of shock on her face. She had just been offered the position of Senior Privacy Director. Her pursuit of excellence had paid off in unexpected ways. Putting her hand up to serve on a project had led to her career advancement. Her aspiration became a reality much faster than she ever expected.

Though the team was geographically dispersed, with Paige on the west coast and the project leader on another, the distance was transparent. Her continual display of showing she was there to help the company and others succeed ultimately advanced her career—the senior leadership recognized a known commodity.

Distance Removed

Excellence takes effort. You will never achieve excellence by sitting still. We are judged by what we accomplish, not by our intentions. While the dinghy effect removes an employee from the ebb and flow of the day-to-day business of the workplace, it can also limit career pathways. You will never be recognized for your work when you are out of sight and out of mind unless you pursue excellence.

Excellence means being your best. It means doing the best you can with the gifts and abilities you have been given. Excellence is not trying to outdo others. It isn't a competition. The pursuit of excellence must be inspired by the right values, priorities, and motives.

To attain excellence is to be superior in performance and quality. Those who advance in their careers are known as people who bring great value to the company and to others.

By volunteering and pursuing excellence, Paige had not only become a known commodity, but she had increased her personal stock value. Other companies have been pursuing her. In fact, one of the largest retail companies in the world offered her an unprecedented salary to join them. In the proverbial "War for Talent," Paige has become a known commodity with high "personal stock value."

War for Talent

One of the greatest benefits of working remotely is the increase of qualified candidates from which a company can choose. Take advantage of an increased pipeline. Create or develop your team with the most excellent candidates.

By eliminating geographical boundaries, it is much easier to find the perfect person to hire for a job. You do not need to relocate them because they can work remotely. You have the potential of hiring worldwide. Not only does the larger talent pool greatly benefit the company, it can bring blessings to emerging economies and third-world countries by enabling people to find gainful employment as remote workers without needing to move. In fact, it isn't even necessary to "bring" the

candidate in for interviews. Some companies have come
up with creative ways to manage the process remotely.

Interviews

My son-in-law is a User Experience/User Interface (UX/
UI) web and graphic designer who was hired by a small
company of about 35 people in size where everyone
works remotely. He was interviewed through video
conferencing.

In the third round of interviews, the company
wanted to see his skills in action. So, they created a
project where he had a predetermined time to design
a product-launch website page. The interviewers
connected with him again via video conferencing, but
this time they had him share his screen and mute his
microphone. They muted their microphones as well
and observed him as he worked.

Michael had three hours to complete the design
project. They worked on other things while keeping
their eyes on him at the same time. Michael's excellent
skills and productivity speed was obvious when in
only 45 minutes he had completed the assignment. He
subsequently landed the job.

Michael's pursuit of excellence makes him the ideal
candidate. For Michael to stay at the top of his game,
especially in UX/UI, he has to continually pursue being
the best. Working with technology means he must
always upgrade his knowledge and skills.

To achieve excellence, organizations need to focus on the growth and development of individuals. This is much easier today than it was in the past, as remote workers have access to top-notch online learning.

Michael likes to learn by what he calls being "YouTube certified." Any time he needs upskilling, to learn a new technique or coding language, he most often goes to YouTube or a similar source like LinkedIn Learning. He can watch a video created by someone who already knows how to complete that skill or task.

This is the age we live in today—using technologies available to us. YouTube is great, but it's only the start. There are other online courses and learning opportunities out there. You can earn stackable credentials through many different avenues.

Next-Generation Learning

To be excellent at what you do requires growing and learning more. Striving for personal excellence and to do your tasks better each time takes constant upgrading of one's knowledge and skills.

Consistently keeping in the habit of learning is imperative. The good news is that it is fairly easy to do if you work remotely. You don't need to "go to classes" or arrange for a group of employees to come on-site. For training and development, you can just go online!

Online courses are offered in most companies, especially for compliance training. Even in remote companies, there are required training obligations. Online courses are able to automatically track who has completed the learning and who has not. When it comes to other courses, where employees want to stretch or learn, there are badge and certificate programs available.

You can stack your credentials and add your certifications to grow or stretch yourself. Adding badges to your resume is the way of next-generation learning.

A large number of senior leaders say that one of the biggest headaches in their organizations is the skills gap created by a world where things are changing so fast. Stackable credentials are the answer.

Stackable credentials can be accumulated over time and move an individual along a career pathway or up a career ladder. A remote worker pursuing excellence can earn credentials that support skill attainment and employment. These credentials stack up on your resume, showing your focus on excellence.

Massive Open Online Courses, otherwise known as MOOCs, are available in many places from very reputable universities. Stanford, MIT, Harvard, and The Open University UK have created platforms that host plenty of courses for you to take on just about any subject. Coursera, Udacity, FutureLearn, Udemy, Canvas, and edX all host excellent courses from undergraduate to postgraduate level, available from universities across the globe. You can take many of these courses for free, but you will need to pay if you want the credit hours. If the desire is for the courses to be recognized by your organization, you need to determine in advance if you want academic credit or corporate recognition of the credential.

Organizations such as the U.S. Distance Learning Association (USDLA), the European Distance and E-Learning Network (EDEN), and the International Council for Open and Distance Education (ICDE) offer excellent resources and places to grow and learn as you network with colleagues around the world.

One of the flexible advantages of working and learning online comes from gaining back the time lost from commuting. When I lived in Dallas before working remotely, the commute on a Sunday into the office was only twenty-seven minutes, but on Monday morning it was an hour and a half. The commute Friday afternoons going home took two-and-a-half hours. Added together, my average time commuting each week was 15-20 hours. These hours could have been spent pursuing stackable credentials like my good friend John was able to do because he didn't commute to an office each day.

John has worked remotely for over twenty years in the telecommunications field. Having worked his way up to a senior director level because of his dedication to excellence, John was still hindered by his lack of a university degree. The CEO of his company informed him that he would never be able to make it to a vice president position or higher because of this. He researched to find a university that let him test out of certain classes, but he still needed 90 college hours to get a degree.

While still working fulltime and being married with two children, John took courses online. His remote schedule allowed him to work, have family time, and to do his coursework from 8 pm to midnight, and then from 4 am to 8 am.

The university program was designed to allow students to take as many courses as they can handle within a 6-month timeframe for one flat fee. You could start at any time within the six months and complete the courses at your own pace as long as it was within that time frame.

Because he already knew this industry, he started taking these courses and was able to complete ninety hours in just six months! It was not easy by any means. John had to write 287 papers in those six months, and worked hard to get through the classes that fast. It was so unheard of that the university brought in a forensic team to be sure he had not cheated by using artificial intelligence, plagiarizing, or having others write papers for him.

But in the end, he did it. He earned his degree. That is the power of what is available to you and your employees. You can take advantage of these online opportunities to excel in personal development and growth. John's focus on excellence paid off.

Keep in mind that excellent online learning is not reading a textbook online and answering questions at the end of the chapter. Excellent next-generation learning has moved way beyond the online learning of thirty years ago.

Many different formats of next-generation learning are available. From virtual reality and holograms, to artificial intelligence and gamification (educational games), next-generation leaders are forging new and amazing trails in technology-enhanced teaching and learning.

Over the last few years, Dr. Susan Aldridge and I created a website to showcase the innovations in online learning. Virtually Inspired is a place where educators can come for inspiration by perusing each video showcase to see how creative professionals around the globe are infusing technology with learning.[7]

Take a look at the website to see how you can wear a virtual reality (VR) headset or VR glasses and virtually walk into the middle of a heart to see how it works. See how you can learn from a virtual simulation experience where you are actively engaged in applying theoretical principles and abstract concepts in courses that are indistinguishable from video games.

So many methods of learning are transforming the next generation of learning. We are able to get information and knowledge in more powerful, faster

---

7   https://virtuallyinspired.org/

ways, allowing it to sink deeper than ever before. Striving for excellence in this new way of doing business is the way to succeed in the remote environment.

Finally, seek feedback from others. Find a developmental accountability partner. Mentor or coach someone. The best way to learn something better is to teach it to someone else. Do not overlook the opportunity to learn from those younger than you. It is called reverse mentoring. I find those fresh out of university, for example, oftentimes have the skills in the latest software and know the hottest podcast avenues.

Pursuing excellence with so much access to learning opportunities will help you expand your abilities beyond eliminating any skills gaps. My friend, Shelia Jagannathan at the World Bank said, "As the fourth industrial revolution rapidly unfolds, the agility to continuously learn, unlearn, and relearn will be the capstone to a successful career." Next-generation learning has moved beyond traditional, degree-driven education to embrace new pathways of flexible, accessible, lifelong learning, and to provide access to everyone. As a remote worker, you can grow as big as you imagine or dream.

Proactive Innovators
While excellence comes with development, and volunteering to take an assignment stretches you to develop new competencies, you can also pursue excellence by proactively innovating.

As the flexibility and autonomy that comes from working remotely increases productivity, it affords us the time to find opportunities to innovate. Proactive innovation comes from looking for opportunities and challenges that inspire you to generate new ideas or create new products and services. But it can also come unexpectedly when striving for excellence.

Most often innovations occur in unexpected places by unexpected people. Proactive innovators at a wall cleaner product plant removed the cleansers and added colors with a nice fresh scent to invent Play-Doh. In 1945, a Raytheon employee working with a microwave-emitting magnetron used in the guts of radar arrays accidentally melted a chocolate bar in his pocket. This proactive innovator invented the microwave oven. A German physicist doing a routine experiment in 1895 unexpectedly invented X-rays.

These people were not looking for this solution. They stumbled upon it. They experimented. Innovation can come from mistakes. It takes nimble learning and situational adaptability. Who is better at this than someone who has adjusted to the remote workstyle?

Remote workers have resilient and agile mindsets. This is perfect for being a proactive innovator. Look at your processes. Work on developing a new product. Offer to take the lead to get a derailed project back on track. Dig to find out what went wrong then find a solution. Use your abilities and remote mindset to seek to find great ideas. As my friend Bret Wells said to me, "Know what is, imagine what it can be, and co-create the future."

Excellence means greatness, being the very best. Focus on what is excellent. Have an excellent spirit in you. Show yourself to be a model of good works. Excel in knowledge and skill. An old proverb says, "Do you see a man skillful in his work? He will stand before kings; he will not stand before obscure men." Working remotely does not mean you have to be out of sight, out of mind. Shine where you are with excellence!

What Now?

A couple of years ago, two of my grandchildren discovered a couple of owlets that had fallen from their nest on our farm. A call to the local raptor rescue center provided the kids with a bit of instructions and encouraged them to learn all they could about great horned owls.

The kids had to create a nesting box and put it on a pedestal so the owls would be safe from predators. Engaging their father's help solved that challenge. Lotus and Marigold, as they were named, adapted just fine, and mama owl kept them fed quite well. The owls grew under the vigilant watch of my grandkids, their mama, and a carefully placed security camera. Eventually they grew big enough to leave the nest and succeed on their own. Lotus and Marigold soared!

In many ways, I see similarities between the owl experience and yours as you have gone through this book. On a fast track to knowing how to work from home or anywhere, you have learned to adjust to a new environment, find your rhythm, and became ready to work remotely.

Just like the owls learned to adapt and engage in a new place, you have learned how to do so from a remote office. With everyone engaged, Lotus, Marigold, and Mama managed the new way of life. You, too, are learning to manage yourself and others. Adapting. Engaging. Managing. Overcoming challenges. Developing. Learning. Flourishing. Achieving excellence. Leaving the traditional environment to soar with excellence. Going from the conventional workstyle to the next-generation workstyle with its freedom and flexibility to a fulfilled life. It doesn't get any better than that!

In this book, we led you through overcoming the fears and challenges of working remotely. Like a catfish, growing as big as you dream is possible in an environment of flexibility and freedom.

We talked about how to define your space and create a remote environment that works for you, while adjusting to a resilient and agile remote mindset.

Like throngs of water striders walking across the surface of the water in perfect precision, we looked at how to find your rhythm. You gained understanding of how to make the distance disappear and how to prevent the Dinghy Effect in order to become fully engaged, and even have fun at a distance. Remote management best practices were shared, like those of Paul Bardack.

We found ways to crush your to-do list. Like caring for a garden by maintaining balanced conditions that yields an abundance of delicious produce, we looked at time management and working remotely with purposeful focus and intentional interruptions. The art of practicing high-powered prioritization was shared, along with deadheading and sufficient excellence to maximize productivity for high-performance-level results.

We have talked about implementing the Bob Ross Approach to produce a masterpiece based in trust, with a solid foundation of core values and a unified vision, along with a strong team, and brilliant execution. The art of becoming a known commodity and a proactive innovator was shared, as well as how to utilize next-generation learning, and to strive for excellence in all you do.

Ultimately, you have learned not only the keys to success when working remotely, but how to soar through **R**eadiness & Rhythm, **E**ngagement, **M**anagement of Self and Team, **O**perating at a High Level of Productivity, **T**rust & Team, and last but not least, **E**xcellence.

COVID-19 drove the necessity to work remotely. It pushed organizations and individuals to try new things—learning to make the best of it. As a result, more and more people took the fast track to learn how to work from home or anywhere. It is a place we would have all reached eventually as this is the next-generation workstyle.

At the beginning, it was trial by fire, without having time to necessarily "do it right." Since things will most likely never go back to the way it was before, it has become critical to learn how to do it right. A taste of working remotely, and seeing the benefits continues to push faster adoption.

Though productivity increased, working remotely without proper preparation had its challenges. Now that you have the value of your previous experience, and the time to do it right, you can use this book to take a more solid approach. As they say, "Once you have good wine, you will not go back to vinegar."

Practicing the principles outlined in this book will help you attain the ideal remote experience: a workplace without complexities, a workflow free from distractions, a work/life balance without the drama, a team without mistrust, and a career free from burnout.

Ideal Remote

The ideal remote work experience is:

- A workplace without complexities
- A workflow free from distractions
- A work/life balance without the drama
- A team without mistrust
- A career free from burnout

Many of us love the freedom and flexibility that working remotely brings. Gaining a healthier lifestyle, enjoying friends and family more often, and being able to travel is priceless. I hope you find your back-porch-swing office and relish a healthy work/life balance.

If you love nature like I do, I expect you will work with such increased productivity that you have time for fun activities and to travel while working remotely. Enjoy working from a café in Paris or while on a train traveling between Budapest and Croatia.

Perhaps you can take a night-safari experience at the Singapore Zoo, or ride in the bucket seat of a 4X4 vehicle on a South African safari. Maybe you will enjoy a behind-the-scenes tour of the Taronga Zoo in Australia, or go diving off of the Great Barrier Reef while you are there. Hopefully you will take the chance to hike at Iguazu Falls on the border of Brazil and Argentina, or see the dancing bears while hiking the Great Wall of China.

All of these are just a few of the experiences I have had when on work trips, thanks to working remotely. I hope you have just as many wonderful experiences as I have been able to enjoy. The world is your remote office.

About the Author

Marci Powell is the President/CEO of Marci Powell & Associates and has been at the forefront of many pioneering advancements in the workplace for the last 25 years. Marci's futurist mindset and thought leadership have enabled her to provide strategic guidance to countless organizations on how to revolutionize the way they work, adapt, and do business in the next-generation workplace.

As an internationally-renowned keynote speaker, business consultant, and author, Marci has worked remotely—enjoying an award-winning and successful career with leadership roles in finance, education, telecommunications, and manufacturing. She has managed globally-diverse teams and inspired over 100,000 leaders, employees, and students across six continents. Marci has worked with industry titans like AT&T, FedEx, NASA, Deloitte, Daimler, and Stryker International, as well as numerous universities, ministries, and small to enterprise-sized businesses across the world.

Focusing on helping organizations grow professionally and innovate their processes, Marci has gained much distinction as a trailblazer in distance education and remote learning and working. Some of her awards include the 2019 U.S. Distance Learning Association (USDLA) Higher Education Innovation award, USDLA Hall of Fame membership, AT&T President's Club, Polycom CEO Award, and she is the second American woman elected to be a European Distance & E-Learning Network (EDEN) Fellow.

When not traveling or working, you can find her enjoying coffee on her back porch or dressed head-to-toe in her Hogwarts house robe with her grandchildren.

Now that you've finished reading *R.E.M.O.T.E.*, I'd love to hear what you thought of it! Please share what you liked, disliked, or how this book has helped you and your company. You can do this by writing a review on *R.E.M.O.T.E.*'s Amazon listing to help other readers find the best book for them.

If you'd like to start a conversation, email me directly at marcimpowell@gmail.com. You can also connect with me via LinkedIn linkedin.com/in/marcipowell, and Twitter @marcimpowell.

For more information, white papers, free eBooks, and additional resources, please visit marcipowell.co/resources/, https://virtuallyinspired.org/resources/, and https://virtuallyinspired.org/.

www.ingramcontent.com/pod-product-compliance
Lightning Source LLC
Chambersburg PA
CBHW071714210326
41597CB00017B/2472